Extreme Ed's Bike Adventures

Dee White
Illustrated by Nahum Ziersch

Contents

Bike Racing

Ed loves **extreme** sports. He dreams of going on bike **adventures**. Ed always has his safety gear.

Ed's Bike Safety Gear

- ☑ a helmet
- ☑ shoes that cover your toes
- ☑ gloves
- ☑ working brakes
- ☑ a horn or bell
- ☑ pads for knees and elbows

When he grows up, Ed wants to ride his bike in a special race in South America. It is the craziest downhill bike race in the world!

Did You Know ?

This bike race takes place in a town called Valparaiso in South America.

The riders zoom down **narrow** streets, over jumps and down steep steps.

Thousands of people come to watch the race and wave at the riders.

Did You Know?

Around 15 000 people watch this race each year.

This crazy race only lasts for three minutes, but it's a wild ride.

BMX Supercross

Ed loves to watch BMX **supercross**. The riders in the race are on BMX bikes. They wear full safety gear.

Whoosh! The riders race down the ramp, over big jumps and around fast corners.

The race is exciting but it lasts for less than one minute!

Did You Know?

The small bumps in the track that look like waves are called "whoops".

BMX supercross racing is an Olympic sport. The first supercross races were at the Beijing Olympics in 2008.

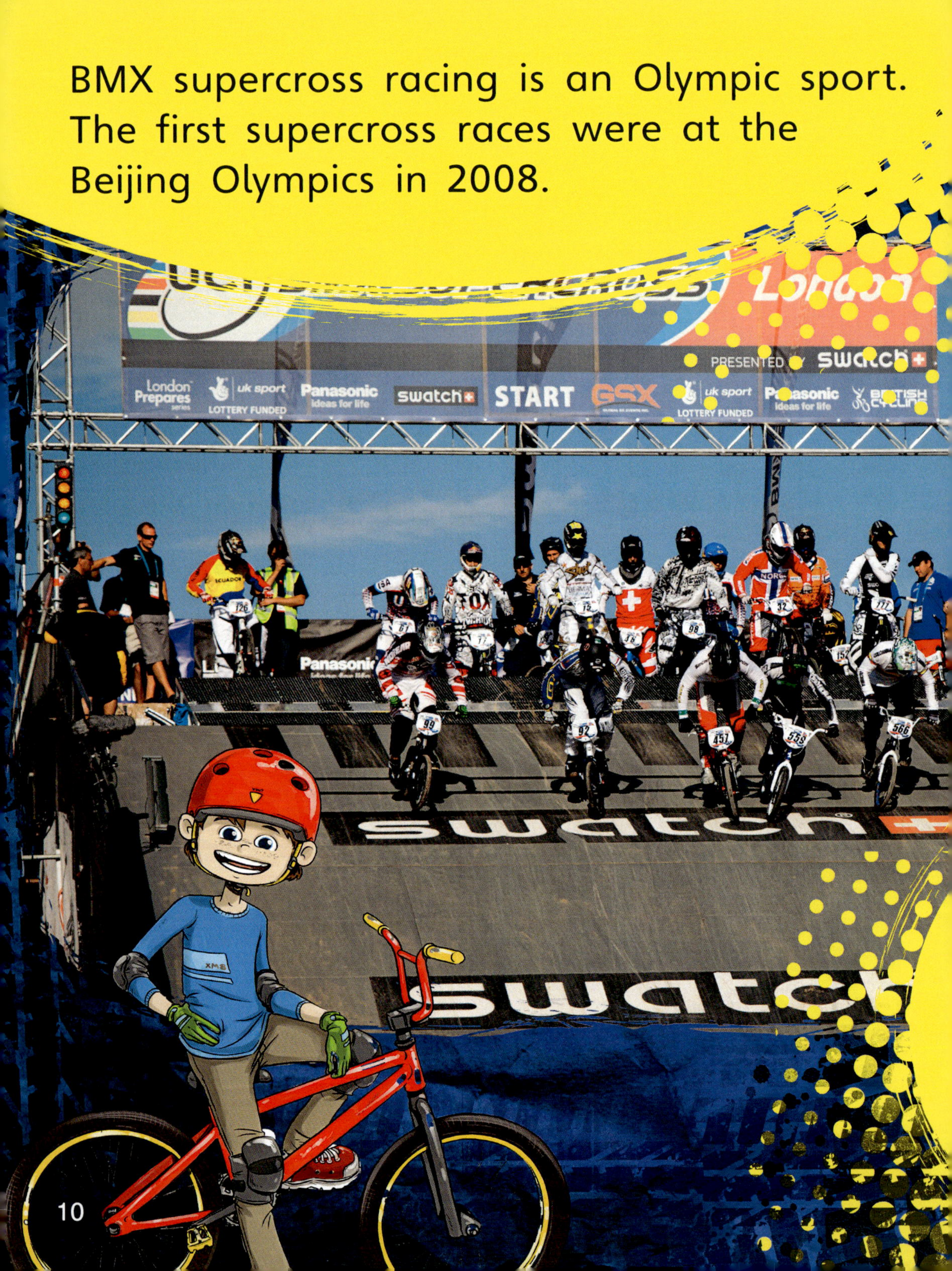

Anne-Caroline Chausson won the first gold medal for BMX racing at the 2008 Olympics. Maris Strombergs won the men's event.

Did You Know?

Anne-Caroline Chausson was a champion downhill bike racer when she was a teenager.

Fourcross

Sometimes, Ed goes to watch his friend Tom race his mountain bike. Tom's bike has four wheels and is called a fourcross.

Tom's arms are strong from pushing his wheelchair. This helps him control his fourcross bike.

Did You Know?

Fourcross racing is downhill four-wheel mountain bike riding.

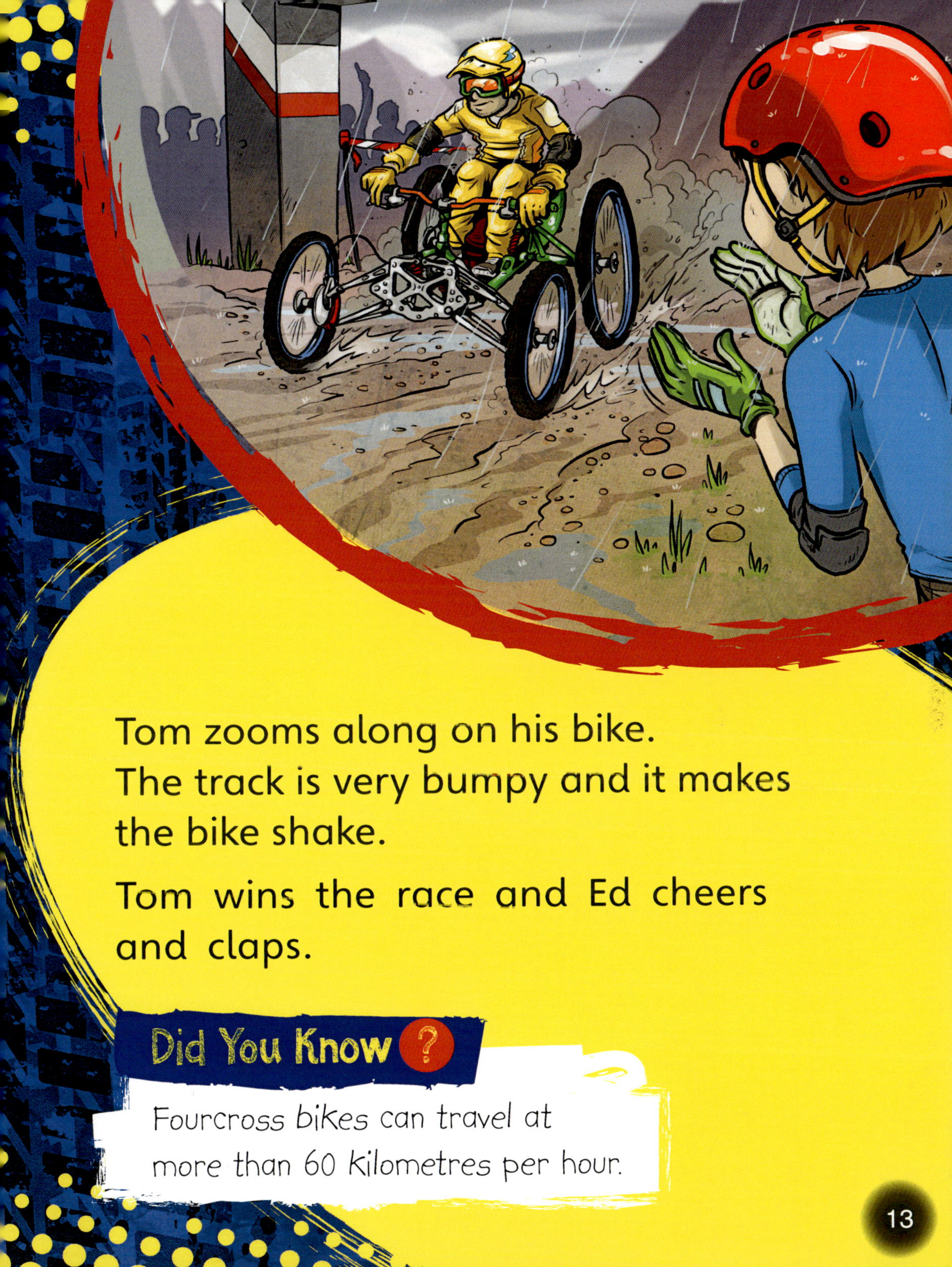

Tom zooms along on his bike.
The track is very bumpy and it makes the bike shake.

Tom wins the race and Ed cheers and claps.

Did You Know?

Fourcross bikes can travel at more than 60 kilometres per hour.

Tom is learning how to do tricks in his wheelchair. He wants to be like Wheelz, a famous athlete from **Nitro Circus**.

Wheelz can do amazing tricks in his wheelchair – front flips, back flips, spins and turns.

Cyclocross

When Ed grows up, he would like to try cyclocross racing. In cyclocross, you ride off-road.

Did You Know?

Cyclocross was invented in France.

Cyclocross riders speed between trees. They ride in water and over jumps.

Did You Know?

Cyclocross started in the early 1900s.

Riders don't just ride their bikes – they carry their bikes over obstacles as part of the race.

When the riders finish the race, they are covered in mud!

Unicycles

Ed is learning to ride a unicycle. It is hard to balance on a unicycle because it only has one wheel.

Ed has seen people do tricks and spins on unicycles. He knows it takes a lot of practice to ride like this.

Some people ride up and down mountains on unicycles. They even go rock jumping!

Para-cycling

Ed's friend Tom also does para-cycling. He is training to take part in the Olympic Games.

Did You Know?

Para-cycling became an Olympic sport in 1984.

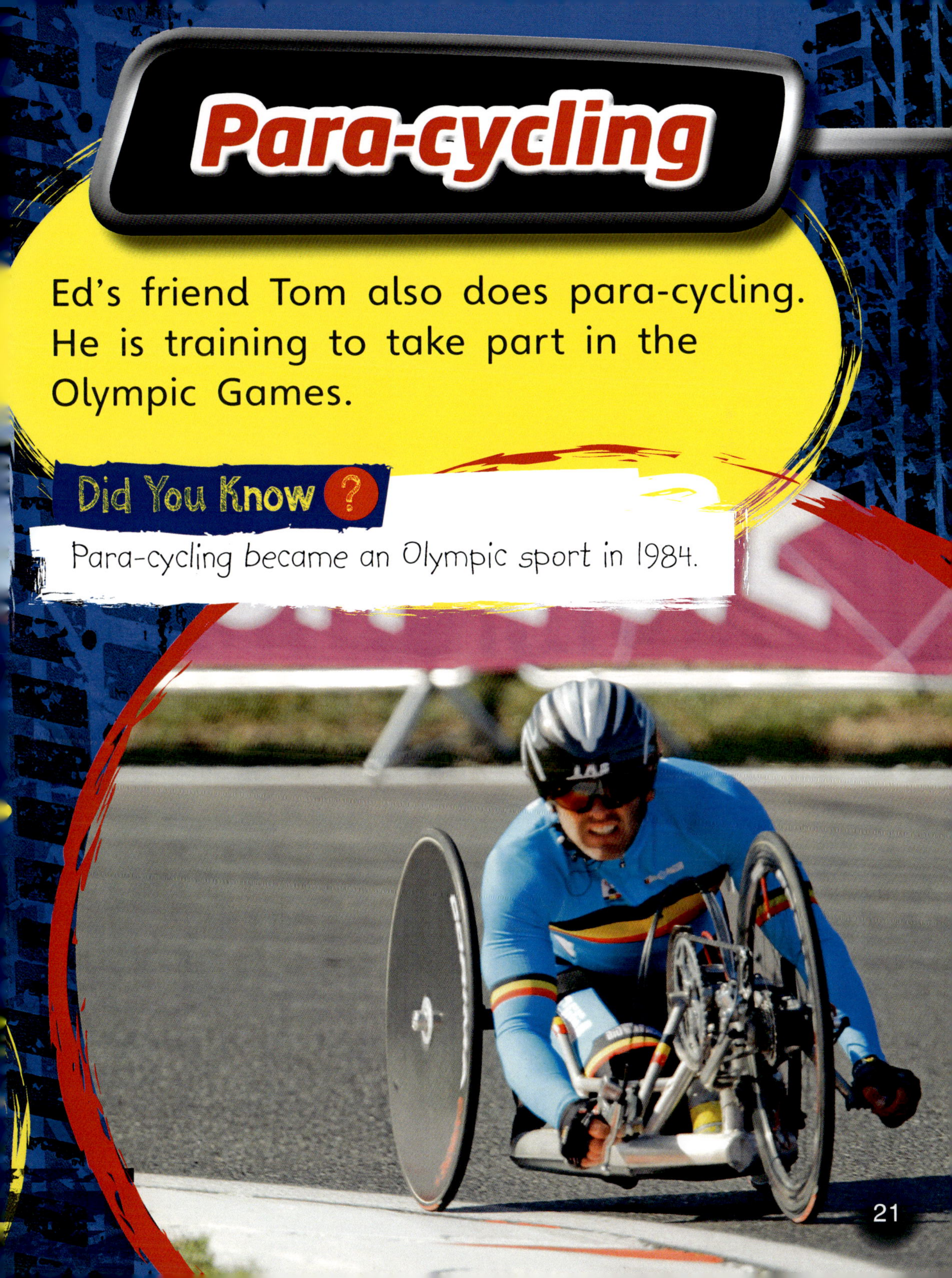

Tom's friend Ava is a blind para-cycler. She rides on bike that has two seats, called a **tandem**.

Ava's partner rides in front because he can see. He is like the pilot. He steers the bike so they don't crash.

Ed loves extreme bike sports.
"Have fun and ride safe," he says.

Glossary

adventures	exciting events
blind	unable to see
BMX	Bicycle Motocross
extreme	going beyond usual limits
flip	turn over
narrow	thin
supercross	bike racing on dirt tracks with jumps
tandem	two things, with one in front of the other